Being Different

A Guide for
Young Empathic Mediums

Shirl Knobloch

• • •

Being Different: A Guide for Young Empathic Mediums

© Shirley Knobloch, 2019

Edited by: Jennifer Sabatelli

Cover and Artwork by: Shirl Knobloch

ISBN 13: 978-0-578-44624-0

• • •

Also By Shirl Knobloch:

Birdsong, Barks, and Banter: Adventures of an Animal Intuitive Reiki Master and Her Home of Misfit Companions

The Returning Ones: A Medium's Memoirs

You're Never Too Old for Fairy Tales

Reenactments from My Heart: Spiritual and Supernatural Civil War Fiction and Poetry

Once Upon a Fairy Tale

Strength of a Lion, Soul of a Lamb: A Collection of Wolfhound Fairy Tales and Poetry

My Ten Legged Journey: The Road to Rainbow Bridge

Waiting for the Next Village Attack: Growing Up Italian, a Jersey Girl Reminisces

Enchanted: Fairy Tales for Old and Young

The Voice of Their Hearts: Learning Animal Communication

● ● ●

Remembering the Magick: Fairy Tales for Those Lost, Found, or Wandering

By Salt Water: Tales of the Sea

Spirit Whispers: A Collection of Ghostly Fairy Tales

Yes, I Knit Blankets for Squirrels: A Fairy Tale Author and Her Bushy-Tailed Friends

Not All Witches Are Cruel, Not All Fairy Princesses Are Kind: A Collection of Witch Fairy Tales

• • •

Also By Shirl Knobloch:

Birdsong, Barks, and Banter: Adventures of an Animal Intuitive Reiki Master and Her Home of Misfit Companions

The Returning Ones: A Medium's Memoirs

You're Never Too Old for Fairy Tales

Reenactments from My Heart: Spiritual and Supernatural Civil War Fiction and Poetry

Once Upon a Fairy Tale

Strength of a Lion, Soul of a Lamb: A Collection of Wolfhound Fairy Tales and Poetry

My Ten Legged Journey: The Road to Rainbow Bridge

Waiting for the Next Village Attack: Growing Up Italian, a Jersey Girl Reminisces

Enchanted: Fairy Tales for Old and Young

The Voice of Their Hearts: Learning Animal Communication

● ● ●

Remembering the Magick: Fairy Tales for Those Lost, Found, or Wandering

By Salt Water: Tales of the Sea

Spirit Whispers: A Collection of Ghostly Fairy Tales

Yes, I Knit Blankets for Squirrels: A Fairy Tale Author and Her Bushy-Tailed Friends

Not All Witches Are Cruel, Not All Fairy Princesses Are Kind: A Collection of Witch Fairy Tales

• • •

"She decided to free herself, dance into the wind, create a new language. And birds fluttered around her, writing 'yes' in the sky."

--Monique Duval

• • •

• • •

Table of Contents

• • •

• • •

Prologue

I knew I was *different* the day I walked into kindergarten. I looked different. I had a witch's nose; my classmates did indeed call me the "Wicked Witch." I felt different, what you might nowadays refer to as an *old soul*. I was smart throughout my school years, smart enough for those seeking answers or seeking my assistance in cheating, yet I was mercilessly teased (upon my refusal of both kinds of requests).

This book idea came in an unusual way. I had written a memoir about my experiences as a medium, and I have been asked to partake in potential workshops for young psychic adults. But my head started contemplating this particular idea when an author in Ireland reached out to me to share my experiences for a young adult fiction story.

There are a lot of young, gifted children and teens out there, like I was. No doubt, the world is more open today—perhaps it is easier to find answers to questions that weren't so discussable back in the '60s (when a young girl like me was in need of them). But there are many who still feel isolated, confused about strange abilities they possess, feeling like outcasts in the world. So, this book will attempt to guide, offer suggestions, and offer warnings about living the most peace-filled energy life possible in this time of scrambled, negative-laden energy in our world.

We all possess these gifts, but a few fortunate souls have kept this connection. We are born with it, but most will lose it as childhood fades. Many of us pay a price for this connection. It is a heavy responsibility on our shoulders. It affects our friendships, our own energy, and it will undoubtedly cause us hurt as well as much fulfillment along the way.

Psychics and mediumship are not to be feared. They are a blessing. But they are a blessing with a double-edged sword. I hope this book marks the beginning of your journey and helps keep the jagged edges of that sword at bay.

Beginnings

I saw my first ghost around the age of eight. I pulled the covers over my head and thought this "thing" was going to drag me out of my bed and take me somewhere horrible. I thought that if I closed my eyes and covered the blankets over my head, this "thing" would think I was dead already and leave my bedroom.

I think now it might have been my grandmother's spirit. I lost both my grandmothers at a very early age, before I got to know them. I think one came in the night to watch over me. At age eight, though, this was the boogie man, a monster. I remember sweating and freezing at the same time, then *knowing* whatever this was, was leaving my room. I could feel it leaving. I heard the most beautiful music I have ever heard in my life. It is music I cannot recreate in my memory; I can only recall how beautiful it was. It was the music of heaven, of paradise, of bliss. I think at that moment, I felt comforted. I knew whatever this was could not be menacing, not with such serene accompaniment. But I still kept my head under the covers until morning.

That morning, I didn't say a word. What would I say? I saw *something* in my room last night. I sort of knew no one would believe me, or I assumed this to be true. I knew my dad wouldn't. My mom, well, there was distance between us, even back then. I am sad for this distance now. I didn't know what my mother might say. Maybe she would have thought I was making it up. Maybe she would have thought it was true, an evil spirit had come to harm. Maybe she would have said it was a kind guardian spirit, simply watching over me as I slept, no reason to fear. How many years of fear would have been eased if she had said that last one, but I never gave her the chance.

My mom would have believed me. In fact, she told relatives about the things I did. I remember I once scared her by telling her something, something she was frightened that I could know. A simple thing, just what happened in the store the day before. But I could see how frightened she was when she asked how I could know such information. I didn't answer her. How could I? I didn't know that answer myself.

I knew I could do things, know things, but I didn't understand why. The world of psychics and mediums wasn't one ordinarily explored during my growing years. I conducted my own learning experiments in the world of telepathy, and when those I sought to communicate thoughts to indeed received them, I kept my mouth shut. After all, if you could tell a parent what you wanted and he or she did it, would you say a word?

If you are young and afraid, talk to someone. If they love you, they won't laugh, and they won't think you are lying. It took me half a lifetime to start talking about things I have seen and heard. I married a man and never once discussed the spirit world with him. It wasn't until decades later, yes decades, as he gradually saw unexplainable things I could do and know. Yes, there were moments. We would argue over a child's choice of friends. I would know the friend was no good; he would side with my child. In the end, it turned out I was right. But as I mention in following chapters, each soul must live and make his or her own mistakes.

I never abused this gift I have, never took advantage of it. I seemed to know this was a cardinal rule for anyone blessed and cursed to have it. I use those terms because it is a double-edged sword. There are wonderful things and not-so-wonderful things about it. I will discuss those further in the chapters that follow. I don't interfere with the paths of others. I don't offer spirit messages unless it is for a close friend and I know his or her reaction will be one of gratitude.

Old souls are born knowing things. We seem to understand that while this is the body we now inhabit, other bodies and other lifetimes have come before. As a child, I didn't fully understand this, but I had glimpses of memories that were not the prettiest. In fact, most of my pasts have not been pretty. There has been confinement, imprisonment, abuse. Those pasts are carried within us. (That is the reason being trapped or confined puts me in panic attack mode. Just being in a closed car with the windows up is a harrowing experience for me. Only someone else with such anxieties would understand. These anxieties might concern water, fire— whatever pasts are harbored inside one's soul, they will show themselves in these manners.)

For me, it was a voice. A mean voice. I cannot place a gender to it, just the feel of it. Harsh words, yelling at me in a dark, confined area. I heard this voice only a handful of times, usually while lying in bed in my room. I knew it wasn't this lifetime, but I knew it was *a* lifetime. Just like the music, I cannot recreate it in my mind's memory. I can only recreate the feeling of unease that poured over me when it came. I have never heard that voice again since becoming an adult. For whatever reason, it was meant only for my childhood ears.

Youthful Experiences

As a young child, I lived through many unexplainable occurrences that I kept to myself. I would hear strange noises during the night, and I would have premonition dreams which often foretold future events. Though decades and decades ago, I still remember these dreams as vividly as if they interrupted last night's slumber.

To this day, I still have visitations from the spirit world in dreams. I never opened up to family members about my abilities, but relatives somehow knew. When a beloved family member crossed, they told me they waited for me to tell them of his or her visit. Then, they knew that family member was at peace.

Family members came to me in dreams, appearing well and happy. They would just come, be present in my dream, offer a loving hug, and depart. That was enough to let me know they were all right. Sometimes they came alone; sometimes other departed relatives joined in the visitation.

As a young woman, I intuitively knew to never try on a black dress in my closet. There was an inner voice letting me know that this was the foretelling of a spirit crossing. Years later, during an ordinary conversation, my aunt happened to mention that her daughter, my cousin, never tried on a black dress. Her reasons were the exact same as mine. Are abilities passed down in families? I believe so. Some in my family have the gift of dreams, some in divination.

Very important moments and messages come to me in dreams. The passageway between realms is most easily navigated in dream states. During my teens, we got a call in the middle of the night that my aunt had died. My dad was overwhelmed; he kept saying it was his *brother* that died, that the call about his brother's wife was only a ruse to get him over to their house. I knew otherwise. I had seen a vision clearly associated with my aunt. It was a very sorrowful passing; she died on the night of my cousin's high school graduation. I kept my mouth shut. I always kept my mouth shut.

To this day, I often find myself still keeping my mouth shut. A couple of years ago, a very dear friend sat with me during a December Gettysburg book signing. He announced his wedding plans for the following autumn. This friend had health issues. At the moment he told me, I got a sudden twinge of sorrow deep within my heart. I wanted to say...*marry her now, don't wait*. Less than two months later, my friend succumbed during what was supposed to be a routine medical procedure. I never saw my friend alive again. Part of me wishes I had said something, but part of me knows I did the only thing I knew best to do, keep my mouth shut. That friend did visit after his death to leave a special, humorous message for his fiancée. It gave her much needed peace and a laugh as well. My friend was like that, always making others smile.

Teen years seemed to heighten my abilities. They say teen years and hormones affect abilities, especially poltergeist and supernatural occurrences. One particular memory has always stayed with me. I liked a boy very much. I found out later he liked me, too, but certain circumstances made it best we never connected other than through close friendship. One day, sitting in my living room, I distinctly saw him dialing a rotary phone. Those of you who are young won't know what a rotary phone is, but I saw his fingers turning the dial with each number. My phone rang. It was him. There was no particular reason for his call. I wished it was to ask me out; he just wanted to chat. We shared a genuine bond. Sometime later, he told me he could not ask me out because he was involved in drugs and would not expose me to such things. I am sure that my father's job as a high-ranking policeman in town influenced his decision, but in part, I truly believe it was because he cared for me. He dated a girl in high school who looked very much like me, with the same classes and likes. It was like a knife in my heart each time I passed them in the hallways of school. I hope his life turned out happily.

During elementary school, I was bullied relentlessly. In high school, where cliques are formed, I never fit in anywhere. I was smart, but I didn't fit in with the snobbish, smart crowd. I didn't fit in with the troublemakers, though some of the troubled, addicted souls were the most genuine. I could be friends with them during school hours, but when school hours finished, I knew our paths would not cross. I spent those after school hours by myself, reading or painting. I suppose that is why I walked a future path of rescuing and adopting unwanted animal misfits; I am trying to rescue their hearts from the loneliness and not belonging mine always felt.

Incidences like the ones mentioned were frequent...knowing when the phone would ring, knowing what would happen, knowing what my mother was asking for and purchasing in the store when I was not with her. Once, I scared the wits out of my mom. I asked her about a particular food, a food not very often seen in those times but very common today. Her mouth dropped. She had asked her butcher about that very same food. As I grew older, I would mention certain names to friends. They would have no clue about them, then return a few days later and say those names had come importantly into their lives.

Once, a friend was cleaning out her parents' house after they crossed. The house was, she thought, almost spotless. I told her to look for the owl. She told me she and her daughter were seated at the kitchen table and happened to look up and see a tiny owl hanging by the front door. They had both missed him. Coincidence? Maybe, but a lot of those coincidences over the years pile up.

Hearing Voices

How do you tell your parents or your friends you hear voices? I kept quiet. Things I saw, things I heard inside my mind, remained my secret. Especially today, when everyone is leery of any "out of the norm" behavior, I can understand hesitation in admitting certain abilities for fear of repercussions.

The best way I can describe the gift of clairaudience is by evoking the feeling you get when you read a book. You don't hear the words, and yet you do—you hear them in your mind as you read. Your voice is conveying their message. The first time I heard my own book read aloud to me on Kindle was a strange experience. They were my words, but a different voice was forming their picture in my mind. Hearing a spirit message is much the same thing, though. A voice, a different voice, speaks in your mind. You hear a message.

Don't ask me to fully understand how this works. I accept it, rather, as a gifted ability that some possess, to be able to tune in to a certain channel playing these audio books. That channel is always playing, and it is always free. Some open their minds and hearts to membership in this audio library, while some never enter the doors of this wondrous place.

Dreams

Spirits find it easiest to enter our unprotected auras in dreams. If you have persistent nightmares, it might be beneficial to practice the protection meditation at the end of this book before sleep. Dreams deliver all kinds of messages to us; they reveal our deepest worries and fears. Keeping a journal is an excellent way to unravel the mysteries in our dreams.

One particular type of dream that mediums have is called a visitation. This is not a dream, but rather a visit from a spirit being. Distinctly different from dreams, spirit visitations do not happen often and are quite a blessing to experience.

Soul Drawing

The cover of this book is an example of soul drawing. The painter applies layers of color on a pane of glass, then that pane is turned over onto a piece of canvas. With hands working and eyes that cannot see the manifesting artwork, it is thought that the inner soul shines through and the paint is moved upon the paper.

This artistic process was extremely revealing for me. Many paintings later, a variety of messages revealed themselves in my creations.

One starts to paint with no clear objective in mind, simply to let what must flow on to the paper appear. The question posed to me in the art class was, "How does being an empath feel?" This self-portrait, with what appears to be a sharp blade piercing my third eye chakra, emerged. Drips of blood pour down, all done in green, which is the color of the heart chakra, where all our grief resides. A being seems to be attempting to climb on the upper right part of the canvas, reaching for the light of my third eye...perhaps my wish to elevate those stuck in darkened regions, or perhaps an emotion *climbing* into my soul, or sadly, maybe the troubled energy of others crawling into my mind.

Many paintings showed dogs, one an extremely prominent wolfhound. This painting class was years before I shared my home with a wolfhound of my own. But dogs fill a large portion of my soul, so it was appropriate they should fill my artwork too.

The art teacher asked me to finish a painting she had begun. She was startled when the painting revealed what filled her thoughts that day. She was also a creative party planner, and she was in the process of planning an important children's event with the theme of elephants. Lo and behold, elephants peered up at her through my canvas.

I am an intuitive, I told her. Now fascinated, she asked me to paint what it was like to absorb the feelings and emotions of others. That is how this painting manifested on the canvas. If I wrote a hundred chapters, they would not say more than these strokes of paint, poured from my soul.

The Library and the Internet

When I was little, I read tons of Nancy Drew mysteries, perhaps trying to unravel the mystery of my own life. Nowadays, young adults have the world at their fingertips. There are countless resources available. Search out reputable sites, and I do mean *reputable*. There are so many charlatans and dark energy motivated groups out there; you must be wise in your choices. There are many claiming to be gifted just because they have the "tools." Spell books and Ouija boards do not make a person gifted. In fact, the reverse is true; those who are gifted will turn away from these things, realizing that the power lies within.

The light of goodness comes from within. The darkness of evil comes from within, as well. But for a young, inexperienced person searching for his or her path, that darkness can come from the outside, too, aided by the help of such tools. I truly believe that these tools are not evil in themselves, but in young, unskilled hands that do possess gifts (and we all possess such gifts), they can amplify those gifts to a harmful and unmanageable level.

It takes years of learning how to protect yourself before you should try to connect and open doorways that you cannot seal up again easily. I still, at times, have struggles with negative energies that set upon me. It is extremely draining and not easy to shuffle off, believe me. There are tools that help facilitate the opening of such doorways. However, my advice is to learn the power of all tools you hold within first, before seeking the assistance of any other.

Nowadays, the Internet is a wealth of blessings in the form of information, but it can also be a curse upon the hearts of empaths. Do not submerge yourself in tragic stories and photos on the Internet. It is too easy to drown in this sorrow. You will absorb the world like a sponge; you have to set boundaries for your own well-being. Now, it is unrealistic to hide your head in the sand. There are tragic stories of human and animal cruelty each minute on the Web. But don't let your head drown in a quicksand of sorrow. The same is true for television news, radio news, and newspapers. Perhaps that is why I was destined to create fairy tales—my empathic heart is always longing for a happy ending.

If you are drawn to work with animals, know this is one of the easiest paths from which to suffer burn out. You cannot save every one. You must find solace in the ones you are able to rescue. Too many rescuers fall prey to this overwhelming sorrow and pay a serious toll on their own health and mental happiness.

Familiarize Yourself with Energy

Mediums work with energy. The best thing you can do to prepare yourself is to learn about energy. Study it in some form. That form will call to you; it will find you. Whether it is yoga, Reiki, Tai Chi—whatever draws your soul is from which you should seek knowledge, in the hands of a skilled teacher. Once you understand that this world is entirely energy, so much of what mystified you will become more easily understood.

Usually, empaths and mediums have larger auras that surround their bodies. This means we need our space. For example, while our friends may feel no discomfort sitting in a concert arena seat, elbows touching the people next to them, we feel invaded. We don't like others touching our space and auras. Combine that with my situation of fearing confinement, and you can understand how a packed elevator ride can be a torture chamber for me.

If you are empathic or intuitive, you will be extremely sensitive to any energy work done to your body. I am a Reiki Master, but I cannot endure Reiki done to me. It feels as though my body is being squeezed in a vice. The energy must be sent distantly or from quite a distance away from my body; the intensity of hands-on work is just too much for me.

As you develop greater gifts, all areas of your sensitivity will heighten. You will become very sensitive to smells. You will have to avoid harsh chemical cleaners. You won't be able to use harsh paints in your home. Chemical reactions will cause you physical distress. Your skin will become more sensitive; even a shirt label will feel like sandpaper against your neck.

What can you do? Well, you can avoid crowded venues, which is not easily accomplished. You will naturally turn to a greener lifestyle, once you understand the connection of all things on this planet via energy. You can start surrounding yourself with light. Make yourself a bubble of light, an impenetrable bubble. Your aura is your force field—surround it with light, with chain mail armor, with whatever makes you comfortable. Keep any unwanted energy carried by others from being absorbed into your own space. Wearing or carrying crystals can help, particularly black ones which will absorb negative energy. If you are very religious, carrying rosary beads offers protection.

As you study energy, you will learn ways to cleanse your aura and energy. Just like you can cleanse your environment with sage, there are techniques to cleanse your own body. Working as a Reiki Master, I had to learn the importance of cleansing and clearing my body after a session with a troubled client. I did not want to bring home the scrambled energy of another. I cannot stress the importance of grounding and clearing one's energy, especially if you wish to help others struggling with a paranormal issue. This work is very demanding and draining on personal energy sources. Entities will use your energy like a battery. There will be times when you will still be drained, even when practicing all the right techniques. Helping others takes a toll on your own energy. It is not something to be taken lightly, nor is it deserving of the many jokes aimed at those who do this work.

Energy in the atmosphere may begin to affect you physically. Some empaths suffer with headaches before an approaching storm. Some can sense when a major event (such as an earthquake) is about to occur. Animals have never lost this ability. As humans, we have progressed in some areas but lost abilities in others. Some of us retain these lost abilities and can tell when *something unusual is coming.*

Energy Vampires

In the supernatural field, the term "energy vampires" refers to people who suck your energy, not your blood.

I am gifted with the ability to read auras. I used to do this for a very nominal fee at paranormal conventions and health fairs. By the end of the evening, I was totally drained. I have come in contact with a few people with such negative energy that they seem to feed off of others to strengthen their own. Once you have been the host of such a draining, you will physically feel it.

You must learn ways of cleansing your own energy. Reiki taught me some. You can use essential oils and home cleansing techniques, but it is best to not put yourself in positions where these "vampires" can zap your strength.

There were only a couple of people I would never consent to as Reiki clients. Their negative energy would be overwhelming for me to absorb and then clear. There was one troubled soul who tried to find safe haven at my Reiki office. She came to a few workshops and classes. Her mere presence had an effect on all others attending class, not just me. The entire office felt her draining energy; even the light fixtures flickered. Others in the class commented on feelings of uneasiness. I had to keep class dates much more private because of her. She wasn't a bad soul, just very troubled and with an energy that had profound effect on everything around her. She even kept her wristwatch in her purse; when she tried to put it on her wrist, the hands would move unstoppingly. I knew that if she ever asked to have a Reiki session, I would have to refuse.

Nature

The trees, the plants, the animals will all become a source of replenishment when your battery is drained. There will be times when the world news, the radio, the Internet will become too much for you. You will be like a sponge, too saturated to hold any more dirty water. Go to water if you can. The sea will become a place of replenishment for many of you, the woods to others. It is here in nature that empaths and mediums ground themselves. We place our feet in the sand, we touch our arms to the trees. They provide the rejuvenation we need.

This is a world of negative energy; if we submerge ourselves in it, we will drown in it like quicksand. We must have that lifeline of nature available as our escape. And there will be times when we must switch off the TV, turn off the computer, and just shut the world out of our aura. That is why many of us surround ourselves with animals, as I have mentioned before. The energy of animals is different from human energy. We do not soak up negative energy from them—their energy is pure and forgiving and filled with love and light.

There is, however, one caution. If you are empathic and work with rescuing animals, the burden of not doing enough can overwhelm you. In trying to save them, it is a very real possibility to lose yourself in sorrow and depression. You must have those lifelines available to replenish and recharge your own batteries. Some may find lifelines in nature, in artistic endeavors, or in the companionship of others who understand how darkness can set upon us.

Comforting Things

I was not allowed to have pets as a child. This is one of my greatest sorrows, for I now understand the comfort and friendship one would have offered me. Instead, I reached for books and paintbrushes. I read and read and read. And when I didn't read, I drew.

If I could offer a word of advice to a young person today, it would be to have a pet. Witches did not have cats as familiars to do their evil deeds; rather, they understood how an animal could offer comfort and love to those shunned by human affection. When I was little, I would open my bedroom window and sing to the birds. My soul was trying to find that elusive melody of serenity for which I longed, in a world of constant bullying to my little body and spirit each and every day at school.

Avoiding Paths to Darkness

Because you don't fit in, you will be attracted to others who don't as well. Not fitting in isn't a bad thing. Some of the most gifted writers, artists, and visionaries never fit the accepted mold. Investigate all that you are drawn to—the ancient religions of the world, the healing ways of the old civilizations—all of this will intrigue you. Darkness will also intrigue. Don't allow the darkness and those who practice evil ways lure you in. Opening doors to dark energy will only harm, not enhance, your gifts. Follow the adage that light always overpowers the dark, and you will have strength to face any encounter in this realm and any other.

Avoiding Places of Troubled Energy

I don't like investigating mental asylums and prisons. If a person's mind is troubled in life, the same will be true upon death. That confusion does not fade; rather, it increases. Some people think it is fun and games to investigate abandoned hospitals and sanitariums. I don't. What has not moved on remains there imprisoned, both by the walls and by their spirit minds.

Because your gifts are enhanced, you have to be aware of using tools to contact spirits. Ouija boards, pendulums, and divining rods are handles that open doorways. For you, those doorways are not sealed shut. Using tools to open doorways may invite energies you wish not to enter. Just as you sense them, they can sense you and your abilities. There are times when I have entered areas of dark energy when I could feel them wanting to draw me in. They could use me. In these areas, you have to stay grounded and strong enough to guard yourself from being taken over by those not invited.

Staying True to Oneself

Do not sell your gifts short. Don't try to be part of cliques or groups because of your gift. Don't be that one asked to tag along on haunted house or cemetery trespasses on a Halloween night. Don't be part of fun séances held by inexperienced people looking for a thrill. You must respect your gifts and respect those in spirit. Calling a spirit in is a lot easier than sending that spirit away. You must understand ways to do both.

Mediums themselves differ on this. Some mediums wish to send every spirit into the light. I don't. If a spirit is where he or she wishes—if remaining near his or her earthly home and family is the path chosen—who am I to direct him or her elsewhere? Now, in the case of a small child searching for a parent, I can see how leading the child to light would be the right course of action. However, some adults don't wish for the light, and that is their choice, not mine, to make. If a spirit causes no harm to the mortals who share his or her space, then I think it perfectly acceptable to welcome and "accept" that spirit. After all, it was his or her home first.

In very specific instances, soldiers still wander battlefields, unaware of their sudden deaths. Mediums may help them realize the reality of their deaths, but I think the decision of walking toward the light is entirely up to them. Some may need time to face that doorway, still laden with guilt over killing another soldier. They may fear the unknown doorway above the loneliness they feel as a wandering soul on the battlefield.

Searching for spirit presence in cemeteries can be dangerous, even in the daytime—and I don't mean because of the spirits. Most spirits aren't lingering among their graves. They are out and about if not at rest in another realm. Cemeteries are lonely places, places where criminal activity can be rampant. You can hone your skills anywhere—in your room, in a quiet garden spot. Spirits are everywhere, but the least likely place you will find them is in a cemetery. I have encountered one, the ghost of a soldier in the Gettysburg Soldiers National Cemetery. This poor lost soul was reaching out to any who could hear his cries. Most often, cemeteries are silent places. I find more spirits in the trees in cemeteries than among the stones.

Don't think using alcohol or drugs will enhance your ability. You need to be extremely focused and able to protect yourself when you do this type of work. Substances that weaken that focus and grounding will be of no good use to you.

Don't trespass on any property that you have not been granted permission to investigate. In Gettysburg, there are strict rules and hours for investigations on the battlefield. Abandoned asylums or old, abandoned, stately homes are usually the targets of paranormal trespassing. This is illegal and dangerous to do. Old buildings contain more than spirits; they also may contain hazardous materials and gaping holes in floors and should not be investigated unless accompanied by a reputable team of researchers.

There are many local paranormal teams in towns. Meet with a local team; see how you fit in with the members. Don't divulge your gifts at first. Instead, go along as a new investigator. If you feel comfortable, then you can start showing your abilities in the field. Ask your local library, too. Many local paranormal teams will ask permission to conduct an investigation in old town libraries at night. The library staff can offer you good advice on their integrity, much more credible than an ordinary Internet search.

I always found it best to keep my personal life personal. In fact, up until the time I wrote my first book, many did not know anything about my work, even members of my family. Some did not understand Reiki. They thought it was the devil's work and cut off contact with me. Some probably have thought my paranormal work to be crazy, though from time to time, these people would inquire about a deceased relative (when they heard I had been visited by him or her in a dream).

Young friends will not understand; it's hard to find a fellow "old soul." Find ways to nourish your own soul. For me, it has always been art and literature, from painting in my room as a child to writing my own books as an adult. Become happy with yourself, which is not an easy thing to do. The love of animals has been of monumental importance in my life. Animals are the gentlest, oldest souls I know. When the hurts of humans take a toll on my heart, it is my animal rescue work that rescues me.

Being an empath or medium is one facet of your life. Your life's journey will have many, many facets and paths. Find those paths that rescue your heart as well.

True Friendships

True friendships are elusive enough. For a medium, they are rare as precious jewels. Most people *want* to hang around someone who sees ghosts flying everywhere. This statement couldn't be further from the truth. I am not always "on," tuning in to the ghost channel. I don't live my life with one foot in the spirit realm and one on the mortal plane. I am leading a normal life, just sprinkled intermittently with messages from another plane.

Friends will call you and ask, *"Is he the one?"* or *"Is he cheating on me?"* I don't answer those types of questions. Each person has his or her own life path to walk; it is not good to interfere with answers. At times, guidance can be given, but even this is walking on treacherous ground. A patch of sinking quicksand may lurk ahead if you try to sway a friend in a "helpful" direction. Each person has to make his or her own mistakes. It is painful to watch if you feel in your heart it is a mistake, but in the end, keeping quiet and being a shoulder to cry on later is the best way to keep a friend.

One of the downsides of gifts is knowing the faces of friends. By that, I mean the true faces of friends. Genuine friends are extremely hard to find for those with abilities. There will be many times when you must put on a smile, even though you sense the falseness of others. Yes, I could open my mouth and be truthful. But I tend to keep silent, pretending not to know the back-stabbing gossip and betrayal of those who smile to my face.

Perhaps my friend JBee taught me a valuable lesson. I wrote about her in my book *The Returning Ones*. She valiantly faced ALS with courage and humor. When she could not speak, she drew a smiley face on her hand for her daughter to see. When she knew she would not be around for too long a time, JBee did a house cleaning, a house cleaning of friends. She only told a few of her condition; she cleared others from her life, the disingenuous ones. I admired her for that.

You will soon learn which friends care more about what you can do (for them) rather than who you are. It hurts—at my age, it still hurts. It always will.

You Are Not God

Have confidence, not ego. No one is infallible. Trust in your abilities but understand no one can be completely accurate all the time. Never tell things that will directly influence a person's life. Their path is their own; they must live it. Telling them only causes trouble as I mentioned before. And you might be wrong and change a life in the process.

When I was a young woman, my mother went to a tea leaf reader. She told me that the reader mentioned me. She started to continue but then stopped herself. "No," she said. "I shouldn't say this." Her saying this bothered me immensely. I didn't pursue it, but her words haunted me. Maybe that is why I keep my mouth shut.

One of my closest friends pursued divination. She was always telling me negative things she *saw* concerning my family. I hated this. Then, she started hinting about what she saw for me. That ended our friendship, a very tough decision for my heart. As I said, I have very few genuine friends. But this is one of my cardinal rules; breaking it is unforgivable.

Shielding

I have been privileged to meet and/or study with some of the most noted mediums. At first, I really didn't understand some of their terseness with the public. People would approach them, desperately seeking a message—a small crumb of communication, a connection with a loved one crossed—and many times, I have watched the mediums say no and the people walk away crestfallen. Now, with wisdom and age, I understand.

There is a closing off, a shielding. One must do it. There is no *special validity* in someone who claims to see "ghosts" constantly over every person's head. This does not make a good medium. Mediums who claim to always be aware of spirits around them must be listened to with a grain of salt (as the saying goes). For true mediums, there must be some intense connection made. Keeping that connection open 24/7 would cause such intense burnout that a medium could not tolerate the drain on personal energy. Your grounding chakra and your third eye chakra must align and keep you centered or you face danger of drifting off into a mentally unbalanced state. I imagine a lot of gifted people ended up in horrid asylums in centuries past.

Do not place credence in anyone who tells you he or she can connect specifically with the person you wish—and do so every time. Spirits come in on their own volition; you may wish to speak with grandma, but a message from your mom's friend Mary might be the one most needed to be sent.

I am a *normal* person. Perhaps I am a little unusual in the work that I do, but that work is only a part of who I am. My closest friends, the few that there are, accept this. We talk about the weather, how we feel, our children...not which ghosts are flying around the room. Any reputable psychic or medium will tell you the same thing. (If a message does happen to come through, I may choose to relay it. My friends often get emails when a message comes through for them. They don't ask me for these messages; I just pass on the intended information because it is the spirit's wish that I do so.)

I hope this fosters a better understanding of those who work with the unseen. Respect their privacy. Don't think that just because they have the ability, they hold this intense energy every hour of the day and night. Time is needed to recharge batteries and replenish strength so the signal can work strongly once again.

Genuine Readings

I have taken many classes and workshops with well-known mediums. I also hosted many local mediums when I had my own Reiki practice and held open gallery reading nights. Make sure you never lose your integrity for the sake of always having something to say. Most mediums are genuine; I think what causes some to make up cold readings is the fear of telling a client nothing is coming through. Sometimes, nothing comes through. I never personally hold gallery readings because I never want to be that person making something up. Not something to hurt, but something to appease a grieving heart. You have all heard the standard lines...*she sees you visiting her grave, she watches you cry...*How could this not be true in most instances? I have seen mediums develop a type of routine, with old reliable messages to fall back upon.

Once, my daughter sat with a local medium who told her to expect a poignant message from her deceased grandmother. The message meant no harm, except I had heard this medium deliver it at least once every gallery session. My daughter took the message to heart. My husband traveled in his profession. That night, he was away on business. About

• • •

midnight, I got in my car and delivered those message items, placing them by my daughter's car in her apartment parking lot. It gave her heart peace. She joyously told my father about my mother's message.

My father, always the skeptic, knew instantly I was the delivery person. I swore him to secrecy. I never told her. Now, decades later, I think she has surmised the real messenger and seen enough genuine spirit miracles in her life to never doubt that communication between realms is real. At the end of my father's life, he began seeing spirits, and I think he finally believed, though they scared him more than soothed.

Never feel fear to say that nothing is coming through. Saying nothing is so much better than tossing a rehearsed line to a mourning heart.

Knowing When to Keep Your Mouth Shut

The one thing I have learned more deeply than any other in this field of work is that you cannot change the path of another. If you sense a boyfriend or girlfriend is the wrong choice for a friend, keep your mouth shut. Know what will happen otherwise? That friend will blame you when the relationship turns sour, saying you influenced the bitter end.

You cannot change a person's path. Watching a friend or family member go down the wrong one can be one of your hardest trials in life. It has happened to me with my own children, advising them against wrong decisions. It caused arguments, blame, and in the end, the hurt was still waiting at the end of their paths.

I also advise you not to do mediumship or intuitive readings for friends. I will never tell someone, even a stranger, bad news. I feel this is very wrong to do. I have lost friends in this kind of work because of this very important issue. This gift bestowed on me has been a heavy responsibility that I never take lightly. Giving guidance to others is a task I have always undertaken with much care and thought and integrity.

While conducting intuitive readings, I never gave out answers. Rather, I always tried to direct one in what I saw as the best direction. Sometimes clients heeded; many times, they didn't and continued on the wrong but necessary paths to learn their own lessons. Sometimes, they returned the next month with the same questions and wondered why things had not changed when they, themselves, had not.

Many times, I have had to turn away those who came back, knowing the help I had given was already all that I could do. I hold my head proudly and can truthfully say I never took advantage of my clients monetarily or took advantage of those in desperation. I never held money in a higher place than what was right.

Throughout the years, I have also given services free of charge to people searching for lost pets. Veterinarians have asked, and I have worked with them in finding lost clients' pets. There is nothing quite so wonderful in knowing a little life was saved from terrible weather or unknown situations because of my help. But this work is also severely hard on my own energy. In the past couple of years, I have connected with lost pets that no longer walk in our Realm. I never tell a client outright that I sense a pet has gone. This is cruel and something I could not inflict on another's heart. I have tried to hint at it, however, saying that I felt the energy was very weak and weakening. I would tell them to be prepared if a loved one does not find his way home again. Sometimes, they understood and accepted. Sometimes, they didn't, and I would later read on social media how they contacted another *communicator*—one who charged very high fees, not working freely as I did, and one who promised them hope. Hope I sensed was not genuine. This has affected me, affected my own energy. I am no longer accepting lost dog requests. I get many, many emails about lost pets, and though it breaks my heart, I can no longer place this heavy energy on my own shoulders.

If you choose to do this type of work professionally, you must learn to respect and value your time. Asking money for sessions is a hard part of this for most of us. However, after years of being taken advantage of by those who didn't truly appreciate the time and energy involved, most of us do charge for our sessions. I have always charged a very affordable fee. I choose not to take advantage of the grief in others, but at the same time, I realize that some compensation is deserved. As time passes and your gifts mature, you will understand this.

• • •

While we are on the topic of when it is best to keep your mouth shut, let me say that I don't broadcast what I do. Depending on your own town and community, others might have a very negative idea of what mediumship entails. Believe it or not, some religions still view it as the Devil's work. Unbelievable, isn't it? But it is true. In my years working, I never revealed what I did to others in the office. If you are job hunting, don't discuss this topic with prospective employers. This is *one facet* of your life; this is not your life. You don't discuss personal matters in the workplace, or at least you shouldn't. Don't unveil what is unnecessary to reveal.

You will also realize that this type of work is not greeted by all with welcoming arms. I own a farmhouse in Gettysburg. Gettysburg is a strange amalgam of residents. There are those fanatically opposed to the idea of ghosts, and there are those who want nothing more than to search for them nightly. Gettysburg draws paranormal enthusiasts from all across the globe—as well as critics who chastise those enthusiasts for wanting to investigate on this hallowed ground.

Again, I keep this place to myself. I have friends here; some are paranormal seekers, while some have nothing good to say about ghost seekers in their town. There are those who laugh to your face, and there are those who snicker behind your back. You must develop a thick skin, which is not an easy task for most empathic people. Snickering hurts, and backstabbing hurts. Keep a close circle of genuine friends to keep your energy replenished. It saddens me to know that some friends walk by my side but then "cross the street" when they see other non ghost-loving friends pass by.

It is hard to find that genuine friend who will stand by your side no matter who is crossing the street. In life, you are extremely lucky to find such a person. They are few and far between. The path of personal silence is easier for me than to confront this issue among so many I know. That personal silence wounds deeply though. I have always found it amazing how some people can mock what mediums do until they lose cherished loved ones. Then, they seek any answers we might offer them.

Bad Experiences

You will have bad experiences in this field. There is good energy, but there is also dark energy. If you situate yourself in places of troubled energy, you place yourself at risk. One of my own bad experiences happened at a paranormal convention I attended. Though the convention was held at a haunted hotel, I truly believe this troubled energy was carried in by one of the attendees. I could feel this energy drain me. It took quite a long time for me to replenish my own energy after this.

You will meet many troubled souls, living souls, in this type of work. Grounding and protection is important, even when not connecting with those who have crossed. When I had my own Reiki practice, several troubled souls came to my workshops and sessions. I could feel the energy of the whole room and the energy of all the other attendees affected by these troubled souls. I would cleanse myself when these workshops were finished; I could feel the lingering effects of their energy still harbored in my office and personal aura.

Crystals That Offer Protection

I prefer deep earth brown or black stones—obsidian, smoky quartz, hematite, onyx. Black stones absorb negativity and protect. Treat your protection stones (and any stones for that matter) with respect and care.

Do not let anyone reach out and touch your stones; in doing so, they leave their energy within. One of my biggest pet peeves is when someone reaches out to touch a pendant or bracelet or ring. Yes, I have had that happen. You can admire a stone, ask what type it is, but do not touch it. I try to back away or tuck my hand out of reach if I sense that action coming. Stones have to be cleansed just like your aura. There are various methods; you can easily find Internet sites that recommend ways to cleanse all. It depends on the stone. Some stones should not be in contact with water. Some people use salt, some bury the stones in dirt, and some use the energy of the moon to cleanse. There are also some crystals that may be used to cleanse others.

Periodically, it is good to cleanse your environment, too. Sage and salt are the ways most familiar, but there are many protective essential oils that may be diffused into your home.

Here again, animals are true friends. Your pets often will sense the immediate presence of an unwelcome guest in your home. From time to time, all homes have wandering spirits that walk through. Most of these spirits are benevolent and are just passing through. Maybe your dog won't climb the stairs to your bedroom for a couple of nights and then be fine about doing it again. You will sense these times—perhaps smell a fleeting fragrance, perhaps the electronics will go a little bonkers. But if you sense something causing conflict— arguments in the atmosphere, something that is causing a heaviness or even physical distress in your environment—then use methods to cleanse both your home and self.

If upon entering a room, you start to feel uneasy, or you actually develop physical ailments, it may be because you are picking up on the energy in that room. All places have energy. When you walk into a home, do you suddenly feel a negative presence? This does not have to be a spirit; it may be residual energy harbored in the walls of the place from a traumatic event or years of arguments and depression by its occupants. Pay attention to gut instincts when meeting new people. Try to surround yourself with positive companions, not those who suck the energy from you and leave you feeling drained and exhausted.

Empathic Pain

There are places in Gettysburg that have caused me physical pain. These are places where a soldier was injured; I can feel where the injury occurred. In one such place, I barely was able to make it down the stairs because my back pain was so intense. The moment I reached the street, my back pain disappeared. Spirit presence can make you feel dizzy, disoriented, and sick to your stomach. You may feel headaches, pressure on your body, or chills and goosebumps all over your body. The expression *all my hairs stood on end* accurately describes when the energy of a spirit moves near. I feel an electrical charge that runs down my entire body when a spirit is close upon me.

During these times, demand your personal space back. Surround yourself with the light meditation exercise, and if you must leave the environment, do so.

The Energy of Objects

There will be times when you pick up an object and sense things about its owner. I have taken workshops in this where objects were traded among attendees. It is really extraordinary to see what can be picked up on, simply by holding the object of another. This is known as psychometry.

I, myself, read auras. I can pick up emotions and physical ailments simply by touching the aura of a person. The aura holds so much within it. Like the walls of a house, or the ring worn by a woman, the aura contains secrets about the individual it surrounds. Sometimes, you may see mediums place their hands on the wall of a house, or on the photo of the former occupant. In this method, they are trying to sense some residual energy and clues about the deceased, former resident.

A Basic Grounding and Protective Meditation

When you attempt to seek out knowledge of another world, you must stay grounded to this one. Connecting with the earth, the trees, the ground itself, will keep you tied to this one emotionally and physically. Not protecting yourself can harm your energy in both these areas. Before you practice any type of spiritual work, begin with a basic grounding ritual that guards your aura.

There are many forms of meditation, and there are many talismans or religious symbols you can wear or carry. This is one basic meditation that you can do quickly. It is not easy, but with practice, you can begin to visualize this protection surrounding you.

You can do this one anywhere. It would be wonderful to be outside and feel the ground, but you can do it while sitting in a chair. Just visualize the earth beneath the floor, beneath the foundation of your house...

Sit in a quiet atmosphere. If you are the kind of person who works best with music playing, then choose a soothing, meditative melody.

Feel the chair. Feel your arms rest upon its arms. Feel your bottom rest upon its seat. Feel your back lean against its back.

Now let go...relax. Let the chair and all that surrounds you in the room lose importance as you imagine your own body becoming a being of pure light. Now connect that pure light's energy to the earth...

Imagine your feet can point beams of light straight through the floor, through the foundation of your house, into the ground llke roots of a tree extending deeper and deeper into the soil.

Imagine your arms are like branches of that tree. Extend the light of your arms into the atmosphere around you. Let that light fill your aura. Let it reach up through the ceiling, through the roof of your house, into the endless sky.

Become a being of light. Ask that only light enter you. If you are very religious, you may call upon Saints, Angels, or whatever religious deity brings protection. Spirit Guides offer much protection; learn to connect with your own guide or guides. Think of these guides as strong bouncers at a club who throw out the unwelcome; they offer help and protection. As you mature, you will develop a close bond with those who are always near to offer protection.

You can develop this meditation further as you learn about chakra points, but in the beginning, visualizing this is more of a challenge than you may think.

In a hurried situation, when you feel the presence of something malevolent around you, just surround yourself with this light as best you can.

When you finish exploring any haunted or troubled locations, you must again do this meditation and ask that your aura be sealed from any darkness entering. This is especially important for mediums to do before sleep, since entry from the spirit world is easiest in the dream state. Most of you reading this have had experiences in dreams or visitations from the other Realm.

Always thank your Spirit Guides or your Guardian Angels or Saints for their help in keeping you safe from negativity.

Gifts Not Lost

You must live your life. There will be college, marriage, children, and during this time, your gifts will be placed on the back burner of your soul. This is natural. They are there, waiting for the right time in life to find you again. Mine found me with Reiki. My Reiki teacher told me that students don't find Reiki, Reiki finds them. I believe this to be true. Don't feel bad if other priorities in life take precedence over pursuing spiritual abilities. There is a right time waiting. You will not lose your gifts. Rather, you will reconnect with them like an old friend.

A Tough but Rewarding Road

Being an empathic medium is not an easy road through life. I lead a quiet life. I always have. My life really hasn't changed much since those kindergarten days. I spend my time reading, drawing, and writing. I have found only a few close friends along the way. Most mediums have trouble finding true friends. We see through the falseness of those who smile to our faces and criticize when our backs are turned.

There were those who tried to get close to me for my "reading of the day." (By this, I mean, what I felt about each move or decision they made.) I don't do these types of readings, as I said before. Gifted souls don't use these gifts on family and friends; they understand the consequences.

There were others in my life who only wanted to know what I felt and saw constantly. Empaths and mediums don't constantly see things above people walking down the street or shopping in the supermarket. If that were the case, our energy would be burnt out within a day. We learn to close it off and become deeply focused when our ability is needed once again.

Of course, there are times when we feel things. An uneasiness about turning down a particular street, an immediate distrust of a certain person whose friendly smile is very deceiving. If you are fortunate, you will have the support of a loving family, and that is the most important element in your life. If that fortune evades you, then animals will become the love and sustenance of your heart. If you are extremely lucky, your life will be filled with both.

You will never fully understand your gift, and you will never fully master it on this earthly plane. Mediums still do not fully understand what happens once this life ends and the next step of our journey begins. It is not for us to fully understand, and what we do will be our own journey for as long as each of us walks in this Realm. You will never really feel like you belong in this Realm; you will feel caught somewhere in a wrinkle of that veil that separates worlds. But I have been truly blessed to have experienced that wrinkle, and I cherish the comfort I have brought to those who have sought my help.

Epilogue

Hopefully, this book has offered some helpful guidance. Pass that guidance along to other young empaths and mediums. If you belong to a paranormal group, perhaps begin a youth workshop for those with interest in the spiritual realm. While they may be too young to go out on night investigations, you can answer questions and help guide them on the right journey. Teach them about the dangers of overwhelming their energy with too much absorbed sadness. You might even help save a young life wishing to end his or her despair in a tragic way.

People make jokes about empaths and intuitive mediums all the time. Perhaps the one I hate most is, *"If she knows things, why doesn't she play the lottery?"* Those with gifts know the answer to this. Our gifts are not used for personal gain; they cannot be. As I wrote earlier, even seeking answers for yourself or close friends can have consequences.

Above all, you must have confidence in your abilities. There will be times when you will not be correct; we are human, after all. There will be times when you sense no answer for a client. Do not create one. I have watched too many mediums, skilled in cold readings, rely on old standards to soothe a client. I have watched them repeat these standards like script to those so gullible and eager to believe anything. Be true to clients and to yourself. Just like any skill, the more you learn and practice, the better you will become. Those that practice deception make the world less accepting for those with genuine abilities.

Each of us comes into this world with unique gifts. Be thankful for yours. If I had my life to do over, would I change much? Just one thing—I would have confided in my mother when I was young and she was still on this earthly plane. I think most of us with unusual abilities hide these, doubting that anyone would understand or believe. Give a loved one a chance. If you don't, you might live with that regret for the rest of your life.

Don't let your abilities rule your life. Live it. Have fun, have friends, raise a family. Don't let the paranormal realm control your life. Let the earthly realm provide all the living you have to accomplish. When children are grown, you will be drawn by your gifts. Seeing family members and friends leave this plane will cause you to set on a quest for answers about the afterlife. As you reach middle age, you will realize that you will never learn all the answers on this realm, but that is the way it is meant to be. Finally, as your years advance, you will come to accept that some wandering souls will remain so and some negative souls must be left alone. Doing mediumship work is very draining on one's energy; youthful bodies tolerate this drain much more easily. Snapping back becomes a more arduous task as one ages, so you must conserve energy and not surround yourself with energy draining people or spirits.

As the years roll by, I am content to be semi-retired from my paranormal research. I still get asked to go on "ghost hunting" expeditions in Gettysburg. Most times, I decline. Now, I wish to let benevolent spirits rest and keep negative spirits as far out of reach as possible. There will come the time when all answers I sought will be provided. One day, you will feel the same as youth fades and the spirit realm draws closer and closer.

I hope this book provides guidance and answers some questions for those who search within its pages.

My Blessings,

Shirl

www.ingramcontent.com/pod-product-compliance
Lightning Source LLC
Chambersburg PA
CBHW031342040426
42443CB00006B/443